CW00707043

ECDL® 5.0

European Computer Driving Licence

Module 7b - Communication

using Outlook 2003

Release ECDL258v1

Published by:

        CiA Training Ltd
        Business & Innovation Centre
        Sunderland Enterprise Park
        Sunderland SR5 2TA
        United Kingdom

        Tel: +44 (0) 191 549 5002
        Fax: +44 (0) 191 549 9005

        E-mail: info@ciatraining.co.uk
        Web: www.ciatraining.co.uk

        ISBN-13: 978 1 86005 684 0

The following information applies <u>only</u> to candidates in Ireland.

Acknowledgements:

        The European Computer Driving Licence is operated in Ireland by ICS Skills, the training and certification body of the Irish Computer Society.
        Candidates using this courseware should register online with ICS Skills through an approved ECDL Test Centre. Without a valid registration, and the allocation of a unique ICS Skills ID number or SkillsCard, no ECDL tests can be taken and no certificate, or any other form of recognition, can be given to a candidate.

        Other ECDL Foundation Certification programmes offered by ICS Skills include Equalskills, ECDL Advanced, ECDL WebStarter, ECDL ImageMaker, EUCIP and Certified Training Professional.

        Contact: ICS Skills
                       Crescent Hall
                       Mount Street Crescent
                       Dublin 2
                       Ireland

        Website: www.ics.ie/skills
        Email: *skills@ics.ie*

First published 2008

Downloading the Data Files

The data associated with these exercises must be downloaded from our website. Go to: ***www.ciatraining.co.uk/data***. Follow the on screen instructions to download the appropriate data files.

By default, the data files will be downloaded to **My Documents \ CIA DATA FILES \ ECDL**.

If you prefer, the data can be supplied on CD at an additional cost. Contact the Sales team at ***info@ciatraining.co.uk***.

Aims

To demonstrate the ability to use an e-mail application on a personal computer. To create and send e-mail and to manage personal Contact Groups and message folders.

Objectives

After completing the guide the user will be able to:

- Understand what e-mail is and know some advantages and disadvantages of its use. Be aware of other communication options; be aware of network etiquette and security considerations when using e-mail

- Create, spell check and send e-mail. Reply to and forward e-mail, handle file attachments and print an e-mail

- Be aware of ways to enhance productivity when working with e-mail software. Organise and manage e-mail

Assessment of Knowledge

At the end of this guide is a section called the **Record of Achievement Matrix**. Before the guide is started it is recommended that the user complete the matrix to measure the level of current knowledge.

Tick boxes are provided for each feature. **1** is for no knowledge, **2** some knowledge and **3** is for competent.

After working through a section, complete the **Record of Achievement** matrix for that section and only when competent in all areas move on to the next section.

Contents

Section 1
Outlook

By the end of this Section you should be able to:

Understand Electronic Messaging and Related Issues

Use Online Help

Use e-mail

Change Screen Display

Close Outlook

To gain an understanding of the above features, work through the **Driving Lessons** in this **Section**.

For each **Driving Lesson**, read the **Park and Read** instructions, without touching the keyboard, then work through the numbered steps of the **Manoeuvres** on the computer. Complete the **Revision Exercise(s)** at the end of the section to test your knowledge.

Driving Lesson 1 - Using E-mail

▣ Park and Read

Today e-mail is an extremely important business tool and many businesses would almost come to a standstill without it. It has obvious advantages over the normal postal system: it is much faster - mail is delivered within seconds. Rather than pay excessive postage for sending paper copies of files through the post or by courier, electronic files can be attached to e-mail messages. All the sender pays is the cost of a local telephone call, or probably a lot less if they have a broadband connection. Consider how much more quickly business documents can be sent overseas using e-mail than by using surface or airmail. A point of note is that some anti-virus software/firewalls prevent certain types of attachment, which contain macros (such as databases) passing through. This is because some viruses use macros to work.

As it is possible to set up an e-mail account that is **web based**, rather than an account linked to a specific computer, messages can be collected and sent from any computer with an Internet connection, anywhere in the world. After having set up your account, it's a simple matter of logging on to send or read your messages. One disadvantage of web based accounts is that disk space is limited. This means that you need to keep an eye on the size of messages in your inbox; it can also prevent messages with large attachments getting through.

Before using e-mail, familiarise yourself with the rules of **netiquette** - network etiquette. Always use accurate and brief subjects in the appropriate field on a message. Keep your messages brief and relevant rather than rambling. Ask before sending large attachments; don't send heated messages (**flames**); don't use all UPPERCASE – it is the same as shouting; when replying, always make sure the subject is still relevant to your reply. Consider the implications very carefully before sending any sensitive information by e-mail. In a work situation, you must familiarise yourself with the e-mail policy in place. Usually, common business rules and regulations state that you must not send messages that might offend, or jokes, etc. Never send "chain letters". Basically only subject matter directly associated with the business should be sent via e-mail.

Make sure your outgoing messages are spelled correctly, just as you would before sending a letter. Many e-mail programs allow you to format messages with different colours, fonts and backgrounds. This provides an opportunity to show some individuality.

Unwanted Messages

Be prepared to receive unwanted e-mails. Certain companies and individuals send out masses of junk mail. You are shown later in the guide how to delete messages, so this should be useful.

Driving Lesson 1 - Continued

However, many of these types of messages have a link near the bottom that allows you to **unsubscribe**, so no further messages will be sent to you. It is always worth scanning the message for something like this.

As was mentioned earlier in the Internet section, be vigilant about e-mail messages; they can contain viruses. Ensure you have up to date anti-virus software installed on your computer. Messages without a subject or from an unknown source should be treated with caution. <u>Save attached files to disk and scan them before opening if you are at all suspicious</u>. If you do open a message attachment that contains a virus, the results can be disastrous for your computer.

To send messages securely (encrypted), you can set them up to be signed digitally. A personal certificate is obtained by the individual to verify his identity and optionally encrypt transmissions. This is called a **digital signature**.

Any message, whether received via e-mail or through the door, which promises riches, prizes, or rewards in return for a cash payment or supplying your bank/credit card details should be regarded with the suspicion it deserves and be deleted or thrown away immediately. Some more subtle tricks have included official-looking e-mails supposedly from banks, etc., asking you to confirm card details and/or PIN numbers. This is known as **phishing**. Delete them. Banks will <u>never</u> ask for such information to be put in an e-mail. Be very careful who you give personal information to – **identity theft** is also a risk with e-mail. Take as much care to protect your privacy while using e-mail as you would in shredding normal mail before putting it in the bin.

On a slightly less serious level, false messages have appeared warning you that you have a virus on your computer and you must delete certain files to remove it. When you do this you find that your computer will no longer function.

Be suspicious of all e-mails from unknown sources. If in doubt, it is a good idea to get a second opinion. Preferably ask someone with experience of Internet and e-mail matters and whose opinion you trust.

Driving Lesson 2 - Using Outlook

▣ Park and Read

For many people who are connected to the Internet, a lot of their online time is spent sending or receiving e-mail messages and there are many applications which will control this function on your computer. *Microsoft Outlook 2003* manages all electronic messages coming to and going from the computer. Messages can easily be composed and sent to any e-mail address; files can be added to a message in a couple of steps.

Microsoft Outlook 2003 is a highly effective information manager, which simplifies the daily organisation of a business or an individual. *Outlook* can transform a paperbound company into an efficient, organised structure.

Outlook allows information to be organised and shared with others. Communication is facilitated by the use of e-mail and meeting scheduling. To aid organisation, all items in *Outlook* are stored by type. For example, all mail messages are stored in the **Inbox** folder and all tasks are stored in the **Tasks** folder. Folders containing *Outlook* items are stored in a single *Outlook* file, so items can be quickly found, categorised and archived.

For the purposes of this Module, only the messaging aspect of *Outlook* will be considered.

If a user is not using *Outlook*, messages are stored for them until they are collected. A very useful feature of the program is the **Address Book**, which stores information about contacts. If a contact's e-mail address is entered here, it saves the need for remembering addresses.

E-mail addresses are needed before a user can send or receive mail. An address consists of:

a **user name** -	the name of the mailbox where the server forwards incoming mail.
an **@ sign** -	separates the user name from the domain name.
a **domain name** -	the address of the computer which sends and receives mail.

॰ Manoeuvres

1. To start *Outlook*, select **Start | All Programs | Microsoft Outlook**.

🛈 *Outlook must be configured before it can be used for the first time. Configuring is simply the term used to describe the supply of user information to the server, who "manages" the mail. Once the required information has been supplied, e-mail can be used. If any problems are encountered when starting the program, contact your IT Administrator, who will be able to configure a personal Outlook profile for you.*

Driving Lesson 2 - Continued

2. Once *Outlook* is opened a **Choose Profile** dialog box may appear requesting information to allow a specified user to log on. If so, select your name from the drop down list.

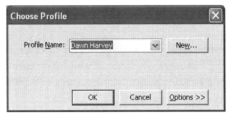

 *There is a Windows option (**Control Panel | Mail | Show Profiles**) to always use a specific profile when starting Outlook. If this option is set, the **Choose Profile** dialog box will not appear.*

3. Click **OK** and the **Outlook Today** screen is displayed as shown below. Many users subsequently change their settings so that the e-mail **Inbox** is the first screen shown.

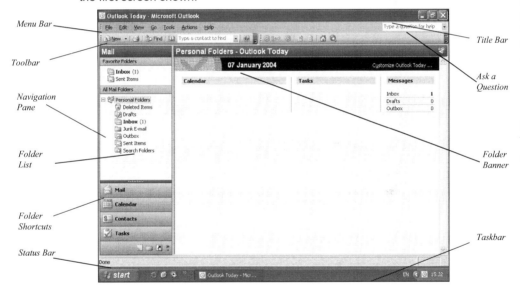

*This diagram shows the **Outlook Today** screen. Your computer may show a different view.*

 *The screen may not look exactly like this as there are many display options available (see Driving Lesson 4). This picture shows the **Navigation Pane** displayed, the **Mail** shortcut selected and the **Outlook Today** screen shown.*

4. Click **Customize Outlook Today** on the **Folder Banner**.

5. There is an option **When starting, go directly to Outlook Today**. If this is unchecked, the **Inbox** will be the first folder shown on starting *Outlook*. Set this option to your own preference and click **Save Changes**.

6. Leave this window open for the next Driving Lesson.

Driving Lesson 3 - E-mail Help

▣ Park and Read

Outlook contains both a conventional and an online **Help** facility, similar to that in *Internet Explorer*, that may assist when certain problems are experienced.

⟲ Manoeuvres

1. Select **Help | Microsoft Office Outlook Help**. The **Help Task Pane** is displayed. Read the options available. Help can be searched for in two ways. Either type keywords into the **Search for** box, or search through the table of contents.

2. Click 🔲 Table of Contents. Notice how the help topics are grouped into sections shown as closed books.

3. Click on a book to display a list of contents, which may be further books or topics. Click a topic to display help text on that topic in a new window.

4. Close the **Help** text window.

5. Use the **Back** button 🔲, on the task pane to return to the starting display.

6. Type **Forward** into the **Search for** box and click **<Enter>**.

7. A list of topics is displayed. Click on **Forward a Contact** to display help text.

ℹ️ *Some of the topics will lead to the Online help system and the text will appear in a browser window.*

8. Close the **Help** text window.

9. Close the **Outlook Help Task Pane**.

10. Close *Internet Explorer*, but leave *Outlook* open.

Driving Lesson 4 - Changing Screen Display

▣ Park and Read

Outlook has a **Navigation Pane** at the left of the screen, which contains shortcuts to various folders, e.g. **Inbox**, **Calendar**, etc. The display changes depending on the folder selected. It is also possible to change the **View**, e.g. to preview the messages or not.

Manoeuvres

1.   Click on the **Calendar** icon, [Calendar], in the **Navigation Pane** at the left of the screen if it is not already being viewed.

2.   The main display changes to show features of the **Calendar** function. Click on the **Mail** icon, [Mail], and the **Navigation Pane** display changes to show all the mail folders.

3.   Click on the other folder icons in the **Navigation Pane** to see the various displays, then select **Mail** again and click on the **Inbox** folder.

4.   Look at the top pane at the right of the screen. By default this contains all messages currently in the **Inbox**. A range of information is displayed for each message as indicated by the headings along the top of the pane. The next Driving Lesson will show how these headings can be altered.

5.   Messages in **bold** type have not been read yet. Those messages which are <u>not</u> bold have been read. To see only messages which have not been read, select **View | Arrange By | Current View | Unread Messages in This Folder**.

6.   Select **View | Arrange By | Current View | Messages** to display all messages again.

7.   Normally, the contents of the selected message in the **Inbox** are previewed in a pane in the lower part of the screen. To hide this **Reading Pane**, select **View | Reading Pane**, then select **Off**.

8.   Redisplay the **Reading Pane** at the bottom of the screen by selecting **View | Reading Pane | Bottom**.

[i] *Some viruses can be activated by previewing incoming messages, so on your own computer it may be advisable to leave the **Reading Pane** switched off.*

9.   Click **View** to see the other screen display options.

10. To remove the **Standard** toolbar, select **View | Toolbars** then click on **Standard**. The toolbar is hidden.

Driving Lesson 4 - Continued

11.   Select **View | Toolbars | Standard** to redisplay the toolbar.

12.   Hide the **Navigation Pane** by selecting **View | Navigation Pane**.

13.   Select **View | Navigation Pane** to display the shortcuts.

14.   In the **Navigation Pane**, the number to the right of the **Inbox** indicates the number of unread messages currently within it. For some folders the number represents the total number of objects within that folder.

15.   To add a new folder to the list select **File | New | Folder**. The **Create New Folder** dialog box is displayed.

16.   Enter the name **Test** for the new folder and make sure **Mail and Post Items** is selected in **Folder contains**.

17.   In **Select where to place the folder**, select **Inbox**, then click **OK**. The new folder is created within the **Inbox**.

18.   To delete the newly created folder, right click on the **Test** folder and select **Delete "Test"** from the menu, then select **Yes** from the prompt.

19.   The **Test** folder is now a subfolder of the **Deleted Items** folder. Repeat the delete procedure from the previous step and the folder will be permanently removed.

Driving Lesson 5 - Message Headings

🅿 Park and Read

The display of message headings in the **Inbox** can be changed to suit the user.

🛣 Manoeuvres

1. To see the available column headings, select **View | Arrange By | Current View | Customize Current View**. The **Customize View: Messages** dialog box is displayed.

2. Click the **Fields** button, Fields....

3. The **Show Fields** dialog box appears with the currently displayed headings shown in the box at the right. Scroll down the list on the left to see which other headings can be displayed.

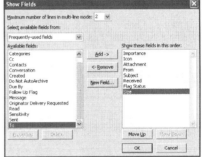

4. Select the **Size** field and click Add ->. If this is already shown, select a different one.

5. Click **OK** and **OK** again. Notice how the message heading **Size** now appears beside the others.

6. Select **View | Arrange By | Current View | Customize Current View** and click **Fields**. Select the **Size** field at the right and click <- Remove.

7. Click **OK** and **OK** again and notice how the message heading has been removed.

8. Display the **Show Fields** dialog box again. To make the date received appear as the first column, click on the field **Received** at the right. This is the date an e-mail is received.

9. Click Move Up until it is at the top of the list. Click **OK** and **OK** again and notice how the message heading has moved in the **Inbox**.

10. To replace the heading in its original location, display the **Show Fields** dialog box and make sure **Received** is highlighted. Click Move Down until **Received** is beneath **Subject** and then click **OK** and **OK** again.

11. Note the positions of the message headings, then remove: **From**, **Subject**, **Received**.

12. Replace the headings in their original positions.

Driving Lesson 6 - Closing Outlook

▣ Park and Read

Outlook can be closed at any time. With a dial up connection make sure the Internet connection is also terminated, if no prompt to disconnect appears. Whilst *Outlook* is disconnected, incoming messages will continue to be received and held, either by your mail service provider or your server. When you next connect, all waiting messages will be passed to your **Inbox**.

⤴ Manoeuvres

1. Click the **Close** button, ⊠, on the **Menu Bar** at the top right corner of the screen.

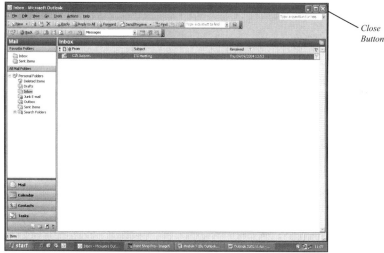

Close Button

ℹ️ *Alternatively, select **File | Exit** from the menu.*

2. If there any messages waiting in the **Outbox** to be sent, the following reminder appears briefly:

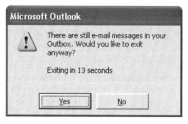

3. Click **Yes** or do nothing and *Outlook* will end (clicking **No** will return to *Outlook*). *Outlook* closes.

Driving Lesson 7 - Revision

This covers the features introduced in this section. Try not to refer to the preceding Driving Lessons while completing it.

1. List some advantages of using e-mail in a business environment.

2. What is **netiquette**?

3. What can gain access to your computer via e-mail messages?

4. What can you do to protect your computer?

5. What is e-mail?

6. What are the three sections of an e-mail address?

7. Start *Outlook*.

8. Hide the **Standard Toolbar** and the **Reading Pane**.

9. Replace the screen elements in their original positions.

10. Close *Outlook*.

 *Check the answers at the back of the guide.*

If you experienced any difficulty completing the Revision, refer back to the Driving Lessons in this section. Then redo the Revision.

Driving Lesson 8 - Revision

This covers the features introduced in this section. Try not to refer to the preceding Driving Lessons while completing it.

1.   Open Outlook.

2.   View the **Show Fields** dialog box.

3.   Note down your current selection of fields from the right side of the dialog box.

4.   View only the following headings in the order stated: **Attachment**, **Follow Up Flag**, **Importance**, **From**, **Received**, **Subject**.

5.   Reorder the message headings as follows: **Attachment**, **Follow Up Flag**, **Importance**, **From**, **Subject**, **Received**.

6.   Change the field headings back to you original settings as noted down in step 3.

7.   Close *Outlook*.

If you experienced any difficulty completing the Revision, refer back to the Driving Lessons in this section. Then redo the Revision.

Once you are confident with the features, complete the Record of Achievement Matrix referring to the section at the end of the guide. Only when competent move on to the next Section.

Section 2
Message Editing

By the end of this Section you should be able to:

Create a Message

Insert and Delete Text

Cut, Copy and Paste Messages

Cut and Paste from Word

Use the Spell Checker

Add a Signature to a Message

To gain an understanding of the above features, work through the **Driving Lessons** in this **Section**.

For each **Driving Lesson**, read the **Park and Read** instructions, without touching the keyboard, then work through the numbered steps of the **Manoeuvres** on the computer. Complete the **Revision Exercise(s)** at the end of the section to test your knowledge.

Driving Lesson 9 - Creating a Message

▣ Park and Read

Outlook allows the user to send an e-mail message to anyone who has an Internet or network connection, as long as his or her address is known. *Microsoft Word* is the default editor for message text.

⌒ Manoeuvres

1. Start *Outlook*, select **Mail**, and select the command **Actions | New Mail Message**. The message window is displayed.

ⓘ *The **New Mail Message** button,* New ▾ , *can also be used to display the message window. If Microsoft Word is not being used as the e-mail editor, a different message window will be displayed, but the principles remain the same.*

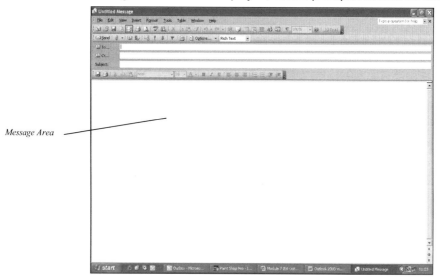

Message Area

2. Type your own e-mail address in the **To...** box.

3. You may also have addresses listed in an **Address Book** (see Driving Lesson 23). Click the **To...** button, To... Double click on any name from the list and click **OK**. The message is now addressed to two people.

ⓘ *See Driving Lesson 16 for other addressing options.*

4. In the **Subject** box, enter **Sending messages**.

Driving Lesson 9 - Continued

5. Type in the following text in the **Message Area** of the window:

    Always remember to check your e-mail regularly!

6. Double click on the word **regularly** to select it, then press **<Delete>**. Insert the new text **at regular intervals throughout the day!**

Methods for inserting, deleting and formatting text in Outlook are the same as in most word processing packages.

7. Press **<Enter>** to start a new line and type **You don't want to miss important messages**.

8. Select the two lines of text. You are going to change their formatting. Click on the **Font** drop down arrow, `Arial ▼` and select **Comic Sans MS**.

9. With the text still highlighted, use the **Font Size** button, `10 ▼`, to change the text to **12pt**. Embolden the text by clicking the **Bold** button, **B**.

10. Change the text to bulleted points by clicking the **Bullets** button, `≔`.

11. Indent the bulleted list to the right by clicking **Increase Indentation**, `≣`.

12. Click **Decrease Indentation**, `≣`, to replace the bullets in their original position.

13. Use the alignment buttons, `≣ ≣ ≣ ≣`, to change the layout of the bullets.

14. Make sure the text is left aligned.

15. Leave the message open for the next Driving Lesson.

Driving Lesson 10 - Cut, Copy and Paste Messages

Park and Read

It is possible to cut, copy and paste text to a different location within a message or to a different message entirely.

Manoeuvres

1. Using the **Sending Messages** e-mail created in the previous Driving Lesson, use click and drag to select the first sentence.

2. From the menu, select **Edit | Copy**, or click [icon] or press <**Ctrl C**>. The original text is left in the message, but a copy of it is now stored on the **Clipboard**.

3. Position the cursor at the end of the text, then press <**Enter**> to create a new line.

4. Click [icon] or select **Edit | Paste** or press <**Ctrl V**>, to paste the copied text from the **Clipboard** into the message where the cursor is flashing.

Cut or copied text remains on the Clipboard until another item is cut or copied. It can be pasted as many times as desired.

5. Now select the first sentence and click [icon] or press <**Ctrl X**>. The text is removed from the message to the **Clipboard**.

6. Position the cursor at the end of the text, press <**Enter**> and **Paste** in the cut text.

7. Minimise the **Sending Message** e-mail and click the **New Mail Message** button, [New icon] from the **Inbox** window. Enter **Pasting** in the **Subject** box.

8. With the cursor in the message area, paste the text. The text from the first message (**Sending Messages**) is pasted into the new message.

9. Click the **Sending Messages** button on the **Taskbar** to redisplay the window.

10. At the end of the message type **Regards** and your name. Copy this new text and use the **Taskbar** to return to the **Pasting** message.

11. Paste in the copied text at the end of the **Pasting** message.

12. Close the **Pasting** message by clicking the **Close** button, [icon], at the right of its **Title Bar**. Select **No** if a prompt to save appears.

13. If necessary, maximise the **Sending Messages** e-mail and close it without saving.

Driving Lesson 11 - Cut, Copy and Paste from Word

▣ Park and Read

It is possible to cut or copy text from a *Word* document and paste it into an e-mail message, so that time is not spent re-entering the same text. If the entire document was to be used in the message, it is more usual to attach the file. This will be discussed in **Section 3**.

↱ Manoeuvres

1. Start *Word* (**Start | All Programs | Microsoft Office Word 2003**).

2. Type in the following text:

   To save myself time, I can use existing text in my Outlook messages.

3. Select the text and click the **Copy** button, 🖺, from *Word's* **Standard Toolbar** or press **<Ctrl C>** to copy the text.

4. Select **File | Exit** to close *Word* selecting **No** if prompted to save.

5. Switch to *Outlook* and start a new message.

6. Click in the **Message** area and click 🖺 or press **<Ctrl V>** to paste in the text created in *Word*.

7. If necessary, add a space at the end of the text and type:

   This text has been pasted in from a word processing application.

8. Click and drag to select **a word processing application**.

9. This text is to be deleted. Press **<Delete>** to remove it.

10. Replace the deleted text with **Microsoft Word**.

11. Close the message <u>without</u> saving.

Driving Lesson 12 - Spell Checker

🅿 Park and Read

Outlook contains a spell-checking feature, which can be used to check spelling of all messages before they are sent.

The spell checker is actually part of a different *Microsoft Office* application, either *Word*, *Excel* or *PowerPoint* and one of these products must be present to make the feature available. The operation of the spell checker is then exactly the same as it is in *Word*, for example.

If none of the required applications is present, this lesson can only be read for information.

Manoeuvres

1.   Create a new message like the one in the diagram below.

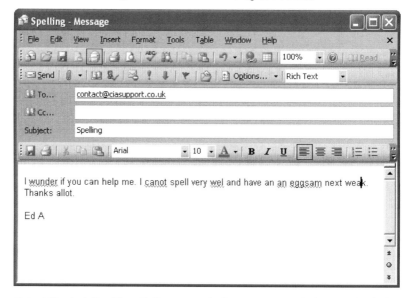

2.   Select **Tools | Spelling & Grammar** in the message window to check the message for errors. If none of the required applications mentioned above is present on the computer, the **Spelling** option will be ghosted.

Driving Lesson 12 - Continued

3. The **Spelling and Grammar** dialog box appears highlighting the first word
    that the spell checker does not recognise. Select the correct choice from
    the **Suggestions** list (wonder).

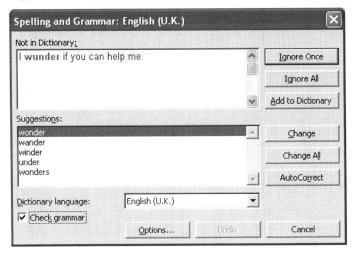

4. Click **Change** to replace the word. Process the remaining errors as they
    are found, either changing or ignoring them.

5. The spell checker will find the duplicated word, not a spelling as such -
    click the **Delete** button in the dialog box to remove one of the duplications.

6. Click **OK** when the message appears to say the check is complete.

7. The spell checker only highlights words that are not in its dictionary. **Weak**
    and **allot** are both incorrect in this context but because they are valid
    words they will not be highlighted. Correct the words manually.

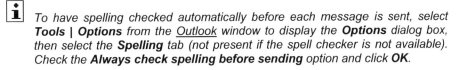

To have spelling checked automatically before each message is sent, select
Tools | Options *from the* <u>*Outlook*</u> *window to display the* ***Options*** *dialog box,*
then select the ***Spelling*** *tab (not present if the spell checker is not available).*
Check the ***Always check spelling before sending*** *option and click* ***OK***.

8. Close the message <u>without</u> saving.

Driving Lesson 13 - Applying a Signature

P Park and Read

A personal signature can be added to the end of a message automatically, without the need for typing it each time. Several signatures can exist within *Outlook* and the appropriate one can be selected for each message.

Manoeuvres

1. To create a signature, select **Tools | Options** and the **Mail Format** tab.

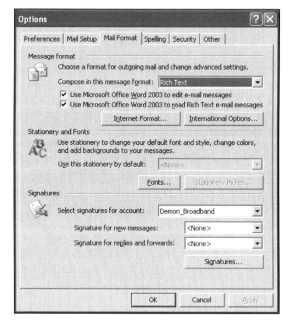

2. Click **Signatures**, then click the **New** button and enter a name for your signature, e.g. **Main signature**.

3. Check the option to **start with a blank signature** and click **Next**.

4. Enter your name as the signature text, and, on the next line, a job title.

5. Highlight your name and click the **Font** button.

6. Scroll down the list of fonts and select **Freestyle Script** (or similar) and a **Size** of **18** point.

7. Click **OK** to see the effect.

Driving Lesson 13 - Continued

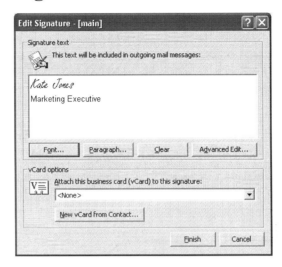

8. Click **Finish**, then **OK** to return to the **Options** dialog box.

9. Make sure the name of the new signature appears in the **Signature for new messages** box so that it automatically appears on new messages.

i *Many signatures can be created and the required one selected in the **Options** box before composing each message.*

10. Click **OK** and then start a new message. The signature automatically appears in the message area.

11. Close the message <u>without</u> saving.

12. To stop the signature appearing, select **Tools | Options** and the **Mail Format** tab.

13. Drop down the list for **Signature for new messages** and select **<None>**.

14. Click **OK**.

15. To delete the signature altogether, select **Tools | Options | Mail Format** and click **Signatures**.

16. Select the signature then click **Remove**, confirming with **Yes** at the prompt. Click **OK** and **OK** again.

i *If Microsoft Word is <u>not</u> used to edit e-mail messages (see the first check box in the **Options** dialog box), signatures can be added to messages manually by selecting **Insert | Autotext | Signatures** from the message window. All available signatures are listed. Selecting one from the list will insert it into the text.*

Driving Lesson 14 - Revision

This covers the features introduced in this section. Try not to refer to the preceding Driving Lessons while completing it.

1.   Compose a new message and address it to a friend.

2.   Enter the subject as **Holiday**.

3.   Enter the following message:

   Dear...

   I've just heard that you're going on holiday to Egypt and will be visiting the Valley of the Kings. Here's something that may interest you.

   Enjoy your holiday.

4.   Press <**Enter**>.

5.   Open the word processing application, *Word*.

6.   Open the **Kingtut** file (located in the **3 Word Processing** folder, a subfolder of **ECDL**).

> ℹ️ *The location is **My Documents\CIA DATA FILES\ECDL\3 Word Processing**.*

7.   Copy the first four paragraphs, then close *Word* <u>without</u> saving.

8.   Paste the text into the e-mail message.

9.   Delete the text **the "boy king", as he is often called,**.

10. Cut **Enjoy your holiday.** from the original message text and paste it at the end of the message after the imported text.

11. Spell check the message.

12. Close the message <u>without</u> saving.

If you experienced any difficulty completing the Revision, refer back to the Driving Lessons in this section. Then redo the Revision.

Driving Lesson 15 - Revision

This covers the features introduced in this section. Try not to refer to the preceding Driving Lessons while completing it.

1. Create an informal signature for yourself, including the job title **System Security Manager**.

2. Start a new message.

3. Address it to a colleague.

4. The subject is **Viruses**.

5. Enter this message:

    I thought I should warn you that e-mail messages can contain viruses. Make sure your anti-virus software is up to date.

6. Make the last sentence a new paragraph, make it bold and underlined.

7. Close the message <u>without</u> saving.

8. Delete your signature from the **Options** dialog box.

If you experienced any difficulty completing the Revision, refer back to the Driving Lessons in this section. Then redo the Revision.

Once you are confident with the features, complete the Record of Achievement Matrix referring to the section at the end of the guide. Only when competent move on to the next Section.

Section 3
Send and Receive

By the end of this Section you should be able to:

Send, Open, Read and Flag Messages

Attach Files

Change Message Priority

Reply to and Forward Messages

Use the Address Book

Create and Use a Distribution List

To gain an understanding of the above features, work through the **Driving Lessons** in this **Section**.

For each **Driving Lesson**, read the **Park and Read** instructions, without touching the keyboard, then work through the numbered steps of the **Manoeuvres** on the computer. Complete the **Revision Exercise(s)** at the end of the section to test your knowledge.

Driving Lesson 16 - Sending Messages

▣ Park and Read

Outlook allows the user to send an e-mail message to anyone on the Internet, as long as his or her address is known.

↱ Manoeuvres

1.   Click [🗋 New ▾] to start a new message.

2.   Enter your own e-mail address in the **To** box, so the message will come back to you and the results of this Driving Lesson can be observed.

3.   In the **Subject** box, enter **Test message**.

4.   A carbon copy of this message can be sent to another recipient who needs to take some action on it. Click in the **Cc** box and type in the e-mail address of a friend.

5.   **Bcc** stands for **blind carbon copy**. To display the **Bcc** box select **View | Bcc Field**.

6.   Use the **Bcc** box to send a copy of a message to someone who needs to know about the original message, but is not required to take any action on it. Other addressees are not aware if a blind carbon copy is sent. Enter a friend's e-mail address in the **Bcc** field (different to the one in the **Cc** box).

7.   Type in the following message text:

     E-mail can be used to catch up with your friends, wherever they are, for the cost of a local telephone call.

8.   Click [📨 Send] to send the message to the **Outbox**. At this point the message may be sent automatically.

9.   If the **Outbox** still shows the message, send it to the server (who then forwards it to its destination), by clicking [📧 Send/Receive ▾]. When this button is clicked, *Outlook* also checks to see if there is any incoming mail.

10. When the message has been sent, click on the **Sent Items** folder within **Mail** on the **Navigation Pane**. A copy of the **Test message** is kept here, as are all sent messages.

ℹ️ *It can sometimes take a few minutes for messages to be received.*

11. Check with your friends that they received the message.

Driving Lesson 17 - Open and Read Messages

▣ Park and Read

Messages are received in the **Inbox** and are shown in bold type, with an unopened envelope icon next to the sender's information, ✉Gillian Atkinson. Once a message has been read, its icon changes to an opened envelope, ✉.

🢅 Manoeuvres

1. Click the **Send/Receive** button, [Send/Receive ▾] and a dialog box will briefly appear to say *Outlook* is checking for new messages.

2. Watch the new messages appear in the message pane. There should be at least one message (**Test message**, sent to yourself earlier).

ℹ *If the message has not arrived, wait for a minute and try **Send and Receive** again.*

3. To read a message, either click it once, then view its contents in the reading pane if available, or double click to see the whole message, including the sender's e-mail address. Click on the **Test message** and read its contents in the reading pane.

4. By default, the message will be marked as read as soon as another message is selected or the display is changed, but this can be changed. Select **Tools | Options** and click the **Other** tab.

5. Click the **Reading Pane** button.

6. The default setting is shown. Selecting **Mark items as read when viewed in the Reading Pane** and setting a **Wait** time will change the way messages are marked as read. Un-checking both of the first two options will mean that messages are never  marked as read by appearing in the **Reading Pane**. Click **Cancel** to leave the setting unchanged.

7. Select **Edit | Mark as Unread** to return the **Test message** to its unopened status. Select **Edit | Mark as Read** to mark it as read again.

8. Double click on the Test message to open it.

9. Close the message by clicking its **Close** button, ☒ or by selecting **File | Close** from the menu.

Driving Lesson 18 - Flagging a Message

▣ Park and Read

Once a message has been read it can be **flagged**. This is useful if further actions need to be carried out on the message, such as a follow up call, reply, etc. You can also add a complete by date to the flag action, which will display a reminder.

⌐ Manoeuvres

1. Select any message in the **Inbox**.

2. To flag the message, open the email by double clicking on it and select the **Follow Up** button from the toolbar, 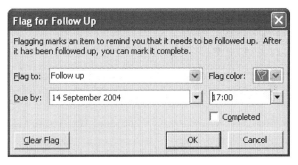. The **Flag for Follow Up** dialog box appears.

3. Click the drop down arrow on **Due by** and select tomorrow's date from the calendar. Select a time of **17:00**.

4. Different colour flags can be assigned to help differentiate between different follow up actions or for any other reason. Click the **Flag color** drop down to see the possibilities, but leave the colour as red.

5. Click **OK**. A flag icon appears at the left of the message.

6. Select a second message from near the bottom of the **Inbox** list and flag it for two days' time.

7. To display the flagged messages together, click the **Sort by : Flag Status** field heading, 🏳.

8. The flag can be removed from any message - select the first flagged message, select **Actions | Follow Up** and click **Clear Flag**.

Driving Lesson 19 - Attaching Files

▣ Park and Read

It is possible to attach any sort of file to an e-mail message in *Outlook,* provided it doesn't exceed the size the destination mailbox will allow (if this is the case the message will be returned undelivered). This makes it easy to send reports, charts, sound files or pictures, for example. When the message reaches its destination, the paperclip icon adjacent to the envelope, ✉ 📎, will let the recipient know there is an attachment.

⤷ Manoeuvres

1.　Within **Inbox**, click the **New Mail Message** button, 📧 New ▾.

2.　Enter a friend's e-mail address in the **To** box and enter the **Subject** as **Attachment**.

3.　In the message area, type the following text:

> **Could you look at the attached file and let me know which wines you want to order for the party next week.**

4.　Click the **Insert File** button, 📎, (or select **Insert | File**) and the **Insert File** dialog box will appear.

5.　From the **Look in** drop down list, select the location **3 Word Processing** (a subfolder of **ECDL**), then click on the **Winelist** file.

6.　Click **Insert**. If the message is being processed in **Rich Text** format, the attachment appears as an icon in the text area.

If the message is being processed in **HTML** format, the attachment appears as an icon on a new line under the **Subject** line.

7.　To attach a second file, repeat steps **4** and **5**, this time selecting the **Banking** file from the same location.

8.　The **Banking** file has been attached in error. To delete this attachment, select it, then press <**Delete**>.

9.　Click **Send**, ▦ Send, to send the message to the **Outbox**.

10.　Click ▦ Send/Receive ▾ to send the message together with its attachment.

ⓘ *Several attachments can be sent with a single message.*

11.　Leave *Outlook* open.

Driving Lesson 20 - Open and Save a File Attachment

 Park and Read

When a message with an attachment is received, it can be opened, saved, or both. You should be aware that some anti-virus protection and firewall software can prevent you receiving certain types of attachment.

If you are connected to a network – in an office for example – it may also have been set up to prevent access to these types of attachment. Typically, problems may occur when receiving files with an **.exe** or **.mdb** extension. These files run scripts and macros in order to function – so do many types of virus. Attachments are a common way for viruses to be introduced to your system. Be very wary of opening any attachment if you are not absolutely sure of its source.

i | *Outlook has certain security settings applied by default too. You can check the settings by selecting **Tools | Options** and the **Security** tab.*

Manoeuvres

1. Within **Inbox**, create a new message and enter your own e-mail address in the **To** box.

2. Enter the subject as **Saving Attachments**.

3. In the message area, type **The attached file may be of interest to you.**

4. As previously shown, attach the **Maneaters** file from the data files folder **3 Word Processing**, a subfolder of **ECDL**.

5. Click ⌈ Send ⌉ , then ⌈ Send/Receive ▾ ⌉ .

6. If the message does not appear after a few seconds click ⌈ Send/Receive ▾ ⌉ again to receive it. The message is displayed in the **Inbox** with an attachment icon.

7. Double click on the message to open it. Attachments are a common source of computer viruses so a security message may be displayed. If so, click **Open**.

Driving Lesson 20 - Continued

8. To open the attachment, right click on the **Maneaters** icon in the message and select **Open** from the shortcut menu (or double click the icon).

9. *Word* starts, displaying the contents of the attached file. Read the file then close *Word*.

10. To save the attachment without opening it (so that it could be checked for viruses for example), right click on the **Maneaters** icon in the message and select **Save As** from the shortcut menu.

11. When the **Save Attachment** dialog box is displayed, ensure that **Save in** shows **My Documents**.

i *If **My Documents** is not shown, click **My Documents**, [My Documents] from the **Places Bar**.*

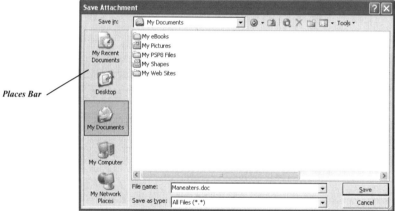

12. Click **Save** to save the attached file (or files).

13. Open *Windows Explorer* and select the **My Documents** folder to see the file.

14. Close *Explorer* and close the message window.

15. Attachments can be saved without opening the message. Make sure the **Saving Attachments** message is selected within **Inbox**. Select **File | Save Attachments**, then **Maneaters.doc**.

i *If more than one attachment is listed, select the required file in turn or click **All Attachments**.*

16. The **Save Attachment** dialog box is displayed. The save procedure could continue as before, but as there already is a saved copy of this file, click **Cancel** to close the dialog box.

Driving Lesson 21 - Changing Message Priority

▣ Park and Read

Messages have **Normal** priority by default, but it is possible to change their importance to either **High** or **Low**. This does not mean that they are sent more quickly or slowly, only that the recipient will be aware of their urgency by an icon at the left of the message.

⌒ Manoeuvres

1.   Start a new message.

2.   Address it to yourself and enter the subject as **Urgent!**

3.   In the message area, type **Don't forget the meeting with the area manager at 2pm today.**

4.   Click **Importance: High,** [!].

5.   Send the message, then after a few seconds, click [Send/Receive ▾].

6.   When the message arrives in the **Inbox**, look at the icon next to it. It should look like this: ! ✉ .

7.   Double click on the message to open it. An information banner appears at the top of the message.

> This message was sent with High importance.

8.   Close the message.

[i] *The process to make a message low priority is the same. Click **Importance: Low,** ⬇. The message will have a low priority icon when it is received, ⬇✉, and when it is opened the bar on the message will look like this:*

> This message was sent with Low importance.

Driving Lesson 22 - Reply to/Forward Messages

▣ Park and Read

A user can reply to the sender of a message, or reply to all the recipients of a message as well as the original sender. A message form will appear where the reply can be entered (the original message can be automatically included for reference). A message can also be forwarded to someone who wasn't on the original send list.

↱ Manoeuvres

1. Within **Inbox**, select the message entitled **Urgent**.

2. Click on the **Reply** button, [⟲ Reply], to display a message form, addressed to the sender of the original message. The original message is displayed.

ⓘ *The **Reply to All** button,* [⟲ Reply to All]*, is used to send the reply to all recipients of the original message.*

3. If you never want the original message to appear in the replies you send, it can be omitted automatically. Minimise the reply message form to activate the main menus and select **Tools | Options** and the **Preferences** tab.

4. Click **E-mail Options** and open the drop down list from **When replying to a message**.

5. Select **Do not include original message**.

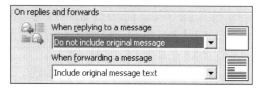

6. Click **OK** then click **OK** again to close the **Options** dialog box.

7. Maximise the **Urgent** message and close it.

8. To see the new settings, click [⟲ Reply] again.

9. Notice how the original message is not included.

10. The **Subject** section begins with **RE:** indicating a reply to a previous message. After **RE:**, delete the existing subject and replace it with **Replying to messages**.

Driving Lesson 22 - Continued

11. Enter the following message text:

    I was aware of the meeting. There is no need for concern, but thank you for your message.

The text appears in blue.

12. Click **Send**, then **Send and Receive**.

13. To change the settings to their usual status, select **Tools | Options** and the **Preferences** tab, click **E-mail Options** and select **Include original message text** for the **replying** option. Click **OK** to confirm the change, then **OK** again.

14. Select the **Urgent** message and click the **Reply** button. The original message is shown but can be deleted manually - use the mouse to highlight the text, then delete it. (This method is used to remove an original message from the current reply only).

15. Close the message window <u>without</u> saving.

16. Select the **Urgent** message again, then click the **Forward** button, Forward. When the message form is displayed, click in **To** and enter a friend's address.

17. The **Subject** section begins with **FW:** indicating a forward message. The forwarding message can be typed in the main window, leaving the original message underneath for reference. In the **Subject** box, enter **Forwarding messages**.

18. In the message area, enter the following text, above the original message:

    This message is forwarded as part of Module 7 of the ECDL.

19. Click **Send**. The message has been forwarded to a friend.

20. Leave *Outlook* open.

Driving Lesson 23 - Address Book

▣ Park and Read

To avoid typing addresses onto every e-mail message, lists of known addresses can be stored by *Outlook* in the Address Book. If *Outlook* is being used on a network a **Post Office Address Book** will be available, listing the details and e-mail addresses of all users on the network. This is maintained by the network administrator. It is also possible for any user to create a personal address book (stored within the **Contacts** folder in *Outlook*), which lists the details of specific, personal contacts.

⤷ Manoeuvres

1. Select **Tools | Address Book** to display the **Address Book**. The **Postoffice Address List** may be displayed by default. It is not possible to add names to this list unless you are an administrator.

2. Click on the drop down arrow for **Show Names from the** and select **Contacts**, if not already selected. This displays details of your own personal address list

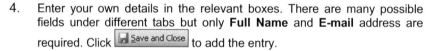

3. To add a new contact, click **New Entry**, 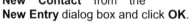. Select **New Contact** from the **New Entry** dialog box and click **OK**.

4. Enter your own details in the relevant boxes. There are many possible fields under different tabs but only **Full Name** and **E-mail** address are required. Click 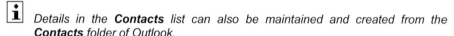 to add the entry.

ⓘ *Details in the* **Contacts** *list can also be maintained and created from the* **Contacts** *folder of Outlook.*

ⓘ *Someone in the* **Post Office Address Book** *can be added to the* **Contacts** *list by selecting their name and clicking the* **Add to Contacts** *button.*

5. In the same way, add the names and details of four friends to the address book.

6. Close the **Address Book**.

Driving Lesson 24 - Add Sender to Address Book

🅿 Park and Read

When a message is received from a contact, there is a quick and easy way to add that contact's details to your address book.

Manoeuvres

1. Double click on one of the messages in your **Inbox** to open it.

2. Move the mouse over their name in the beige area after **From** and right click.

3. Select **Add to Outlook Contacts** from the shortcut menu. When the contact form appears, add any further details that may be required, then click **Save and Close**.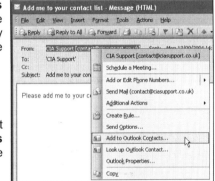

4. Close the message.

5. Open the **Address Book**, select **Show Names from... Contacts** and scroll down the list to see the new entry.

6. Close the **Address Book**.

7. The contact that was just added to the address book has decided to move to a deserted island, without leaving a forwarding address. Open the **Address Book** again.

8. Select the contact. To delete this mail address from the list, click the **Delete** button, ☒, on the toolbar of the **Address Book**.

9. Click **Yes** at the prompt to delete the contact's details.

10. Close the **Address Book**, but leave the **Inbox** open.

Driving Lesson 25 - Distribution Lists

▣ Park and Read

It is possible to create **Distribution Lists** of specific contacts, so that messages can be sent to groups of people with a single click of the mouse. Multiple distribution lists can be created, each containing particular types of contact, such as family, darts team, friends, etc. Any contact can belong to more than one list.

⌇ Manoeuvres

1. To create a distribution list from an existing address book, open the **Address Book**. Click the **New Entry** button, ▦ and select **New Distribution List**.

2. Click **OK** to display the **Untitled - Distribution List** dialog box and maximise it if necessary.

3. Enter **Friends** in the **Name** box. This is the name of the distribution list.

4. Click **Select Members**. Make sure **Contacts** is selected in the top drop down box, then double click on a name from the list, to add them to the list of **Members**.

☐ *Names can be added from the **Postoffice Address** list by changing the **Show Names from the** option at the top of the dialog box.*

5. Add two more friends to the list of **Members**, then click **OK**.

Driving Lesson 25 - Continued

6. The **Friends Distribution List** window is displayed.

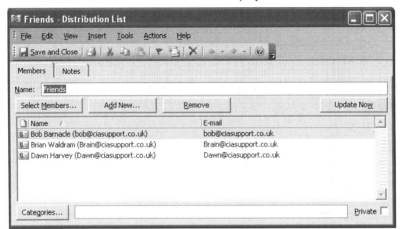

 *Members can be added, amended or removed using this screen. To remove a member from the list, highlight the name and click **Remove**.*

7. Click **Save and Close**. The **Friends** distribution group is added to the **Contacts Address Book**. Display the **Contacts** list to see it.

Dawn Harvey	Dawn Harvey (Dawn…
Friends	**Friends**
Terrence Charlton	Terrence Charlton (T…

8. Close the address book and compose a new message. To send the message to everyone on the **Friends** distribution list, click on 🔲 To… .

9. Select **Contacts** from **Show Names** … double click on **Friends** from the list, then click **OK**.

10. This message will be sent to all friends who have been added to the distribution list. Enter the subject as **Distribution Lists**.

11. Type in a suitable message and send it.

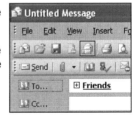

 *Once the message is sent, all the individual addresses in the distribution list will be shown the **To** address box.*

 *To send the same message to several people in the address book who are not on a distribution list, click 🔲 To… , then double click on each required name, before clicking **OK**.*

Driving Lesson 26 - Revision

This covers the features introduced in this section. Try not to refer to the preceding Driving Lessons while completing it.

1. Check for any new messages in the **Inbox**.

2. Read any that may have arrived.

3. Select any single message that has been read and mark it as unread.

4. Flag the selected message for one week's time.

5. Remove the flag.

6. Close any open messages.

7. Open the **Contacts Address Book** and add three new entries, using the names and addresses of colleagues.

8. Create a new distribution list in **Contacts**, named **Colleagues** and select the new entries as **Members**.

9. Address the message to the **Colleagues** distribution list and enter the subject as **Diet**.

10. Attach the file **Calories** (located in the **4 Spreadsheets** folder, a subfolder of **ECDL**).

11. Enter the message text as follows:

    I thought this calorie counter might be useful for those of us starting the new wonder diet.

12. Make the message **High Priority** and send it.

If you experienced any difficulty completing the Revision, refer back to the Driving Lessons in this section. Then redo the Revision.

Driving Lesson 27 - Revision

This covers the features introduced in this section. Try not to refer to the preceding Driving Lessons while completing it.

1.   Start a new message and address it to yourself.

2.   Send a copy to a friend or colleague.

3.   Enter the **Subject** as **Web Page**.

4.   Attach the file **Images** that was saved in **My Documents** in the Internet section. If you do not have this file choose any other.

5.   Enter the body of the message as **Have a look at the web site in the attached file**.

6.   Send the message.

7.   After a minute check for incoming mail.

8.   When the **Web Page** message arrives save the attachment in **My Documents**.

9.   Overwrite the original file if prompted, as the attachment is exactly the same.

If you experienced any difficulty completing the Revision, refer back to the Driving Lessons in this section. Then redo the Revision.

Driving Lesson 28 - Revision

This covers the features introduced in this section. Try not to refer to the preceding Driving Lessons while completing it.

1.   Create a distribution list named **Staff** in the **Contacts** address book.

2.   Add three friends or colleagues to the list.

3.   Create a new message.

4.   Address the message to the **Staff** distribution list.

5.   Send a carbon copy to yourself.

6.   Enter the **Subject** as **Team Building Trip**.

7.   Make the message high priority.

8.   Enter the following message:

> **This month's outing is to a local paint balling range. Please let me know if you are free on Friday week.**

9.   Send the message.

10. Check for incoming mail.

11. Flag the **Team Building Trip** message.

12. Reply to the message, saying that you are free.

13. Send the message.

If you experienced any difficulty completing the Revision, refer back to the Driving Lessons in this section. Then redo the Revision.

Once you are confident with the features, complete the Record of Achievement Matrix referring to the section at the end of the guide. Only when competent move on to the next Section.

Section 4 Message Management

By the end of this Section you should be able to:

Save a Draft Message

Print Messages

Delete Messages

Organise Messages in Folders

To gain an understanding of the above features, work through the **Driving Lessons** in this **Section**.

For each **Driving Lesson**, read the **Park and Read** instructions, without touching the keyboard, then work through the numbered steps of the **Manoeuvres** on the computer. Complete the **Revision Exercise(s)** at the end of the section to test your knowledge.

Driving Lesson 29 - Save a Draft Message

▣ Park and Read

Occasionally, you may be in the middle of typing a message when you have to leave it, perhaps to check information. This doesn't mean the message is lost - you can save a draft copy and come back to it later.

↱ Manoeuvres

1. Within **Inbox**, start a new message with the subject **Meeting**.

2. Type in the message **Are you available for the staffing meeting on**.

3. You need to check the date of the meeting. Click the **Close** button on the message. The following prompt appears:

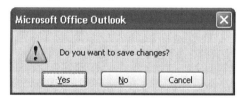

4. Click **Yes**. The information message shows it's been saved.

ℹ️ *Alternatively to save to* ***Drafts*** *select* ***File | Save*** *or press* ***<Ctrl S>*** *and then* ***Close*** *the message.*

5. Click **OK** if the above message is displayed.

6. Notice the **Drafts** icon, 🗐 **Drafts** (1) , in the **Folder List**, showing there is a single draft message.

ℹ️ *To continue a draft message at a later stage, click the* ***Drafts*** *folder. Double click on the message to open it and continue as usual.*

Driving Lesson 30 - Printing a Message

▣ Park and Read

Messages can be printed by simply opening the desired message, then selecting the print command. The number of copies and print range can be selected as required.

⌒ Manoeuvres

1. Within **Inbox**, open the e-mail **Urgent** by double clicking it.

2. Select **File | Print** or press **<Ctrl P>**. The **Print** dialog box is displayed. This is different depending on the format of the received message; the one below is for **HTML** messages.

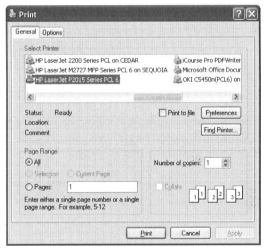

ℹ️ *If the received message is in **RTF** or **Plain Text** format, the **Print** dialog box is different. It includes a **Preview** button to preview messages before printing but doesn't allow part of a message to be printed. These types of messages can also be previewed using the **File | Print Preview** menu.*

3. In **Number of** copies, use the up spinner to increase the number to **2**. Click **OK** to print two copies of the e-mail.

ℹ️ *There are options to print specified pages via the **Pages** box, or just a highlighted part of text via **Selection** of **HTML** messages.*

4. Select a different message from the **Inbox**.

5. Click the 🖨 button to print one copy of the entire e-message to the default printer.

6. Close the message, but leave the **Inbox** open.

Driving Lesson 31 - Deleting Messages

▣ Park and Read

All messages received are stored in the **Inbox**. After a period of time these messages will need to be deleted. Once selected, messages can be deleted and are moved from the **Inbox** to the **Deleted Items** folder, a temporary store, until confirmation of permanent deletion.

⌐ Manoeuvres

1. In the **Inbox**, select the **Test message**.

> ℹ️ *To select all messages, press <**Ctrl A**>, to select non adjacent messages hold the <**Ctrl**> key and click the required messages, to select a range, use the <**Shift**> key.*

2. Click the ☒ button on the toolbar and the message is deleted.

3. Scroll down the **Folder List** and select 🗑 Deleted Items . The information viewer will now show all deleted messages.

4. To retrieve the **Test message** and replace it in the **Inbox**, right click on it, then select **Move to Folder**. From the list in the **Move Items** dialog box, select **Inbox**, then click **OK**.

> ℹ️ *A deleted message can also be clicked and dragged from where it is being viewed in the **Deleted Items** folder, to the required folder on the **Folder List**.*

5. View the **Inbox** folder to see that the message has been retrieved.

6. Delete the message again, but this time use the <**Delete**> key, which is an alternative method.

7. View the **Deleted Items** folder; the message has reappeared.

8. To empty the **Deleted Items** folder, right click 🗑 Deleted Items and select **Empty "Deleted Items" Folder** from the menu.

9. In the **Warning message** box, select **Yes** and the messages will be permanently deleted.

Driving Lesson 32 - Creating Inbox Folders

▣ Park and Read

If the same computer is being used by several people, it may be a good idea to create a system of folders in which to store their individual messages. Once folders have been set up, messages can be sent directly to them on receipt. Messages can be moved between folders as required. Unwanted folders can be deleted.

☞ Manoeuvres

1. To create your own mail folder within the **Inbox**, first make sure the **Inbox** is selected and then select **File | Folder | New Folder**.

2. In the **Name** box, type in your first name and click **OK**.

3. If there is a prompt to add a shortcut to your **Outlook Bar** click **No**.

4. Look at the **Folder List**. The new folder has been created as a subfolder of the **Inbox**. If the structure within **Inbox** is ever hidden, click on the plus sign at the left, ⊞ 🖾 Inbox, to display it.

ℹ️ *Folders can be created within any of the displayed folders.*

ℹ️ *To delete a folder, right click on it and select **Delete** "Folder Name".*

Driving Lesson 32 - Continued

5.   To arrange for your incoming mail to be sent to the new folder, select **Tools | Rules and Alerts** then click **New Rule** button in the **Rules and Alerts** dialog box. Close the **Office Assistant** if it appears.

6.   Ensure **Start creating a rule from a template** is selected, then select **Move messages with specific words in the subject to a folder** from the list.

7.   Click **Next**, uncheck the existing **Condition** selections then check **where my name is in the To or Cc box**.

8.   Click **Next**, ensure that **move it to the specified folder** is selected from the **Actions** list. In the **Rule description** area, click on the word **specified**. In the **Choose a folder** list, expand the **Inbox** by clicking on the **+** sign to the left and select your folder. Click **OK**.

9.   Click **Next**, do not select any exceptions and click **Next** again.

10.   In **Please specify a name for this rule**, type **Forward My Mail** and click **Finish**.

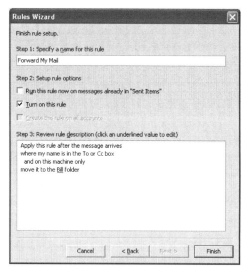

11.   Click **OK** again to complete the process. <u>This means that all incoming mail addressed to you will be moved to the new folder, not the **Inbox**.</u>

12.   Test the rule by receiving messages for the person named in the rule and checking that they are routed to the designated folder.

13.   Select **Tools | Rules and Alerts**, display the **Rules Wizard** dialog box, and select the rule just created and click **Delete** (removing the tick from the entry would deactivate the rule without deleting it). Click **Yes** to confirm the deletion then click **OK** to close the dialog box.

Driving Lesson 33 - Organising Messages

 Park and Read

Once folders have been created, messages can be moved between them if necessary. It is also possible to sort messages in various ways.

Manoeuvres

1.   Make sure the **Inbox** is the folder being viewed.

2.   To sort the messages by name of sender, click on the **From** heading at the top of the message pane.

3.   To sort the messages by date and time received, click on the **Received** heading. The default order is to show the most recent first. This is useful as new messages will always appear at the top. Click the heading again to sort them in the reverse date order, then click again to restore the default order.

> **i** *Messages can be sorted by **Importance**, **Attachment**, **Size** and **Subject** in the same way (ensure all message headings are displayed, see DL 44).*

4.   Select any message from the **Inbox**. To move it to your folder, first make sure that your folder is visible in the **Navigation Pane**. Right click on the message and select **Move to Folder** from the shortcut menu.

5.   Select your folder in the **Move Items** dialog box and click **OK**. The message has been moved. Open your folder to check.

> **i** *Messages can also be moved to any folder on the **Folder List** by clicking and dragging.*

6.   In the **Inbox**, sort all the messages by date received, with the most recently received messages at the top.

7.   Select your folder in the **Folder List** and press <**Delete**>. A confirmation box is displayed.

8.   Click **Yes**. In the **Folders List**, your folder is now shown within the **Deleted Items** folder.

9.   Select your folder from within **Deleted Items** and press <**Delete**>. Another box is displayed to confirm the permanent deletion of the folder. Select **Yes** and the folder is removed from the computer.

Driving Lesson 34 - Finding Messages

▣ Park and Read

It is also possible to search for messages in various ways. For example, messages from a particular person, with a specific subject or content.

↱ Manoeuvres

1. Make sure the **Inbox** is displayed. To search for a message, click the **Find** button, 🔍 Find.

2. The **Find** bar appears.

3. Enter your name in the **Look for** box, then click **Find Now**. After a few seconds, a list of messages received from you should appear in the **Message pane**.

ℹ *The default search option is to search all of the text in the messages for a match so the above example would also find any messages where your name appeared in the message text as well as in the From field.*

4. Double click on a message to open it.

5. Close the message but leave the **Find** bar open.

6. Click **Clear** on the **Find** bar. The **Look for** box will be cleared and a complete list of messages will be restored in the **Message pane**.

ℹ *Advanced options allow searches to made on specific headings. If a consistent system of labelling **Subjects** on messages is used, it will be possible to search for all messages relating to a particular subject.*

7. This time, to search for messages with a specific subject, click the **Options** drop down arrow on the **Find** bar and select **Advanced Find**.

8. At the top of the **Advanced Find** dialog box make sure the **Look for** box contains **Messages** then click the **Browse** button.

9. View the folders in the **Select Folders** dialog box and make sure that only **Inbox** has a check mark. Click **OK**.

Driving Lesson 34 - Continued

10. With the **Messages** tab selected, enter **attachments** in the **Search for the word(s)** box. In the **In** box below this, make sure **subject field only** is selected.

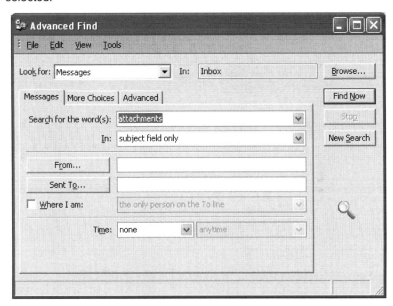

11. Click **Find Now**. These criteria will search for any **Messages** in the **Inbox** containing the word **attachments** in the **Subject** field.

12. Notice the message(s) displayed at the bottom of the box.

13. Click **New Search**, then **OK** at the prompt.

14. To find any messages about the area manager, type **area manager** in the **Search for the word(s)** box.

15. From the **In** drop down list select **subject field and message body**.

16. Click **Find Now**. There should be at least one message, with the subject **Urgent**.

17. Double click on the message to open it. Check for the text **area manager**.

18. Close the message and the **Advanced Find** dialog box.

19. Click the **Find** button on the toolbar to close the **Find** bar.

Driving Lesson 35 - Revision

This covers the features introduced in this section. Try not to refer to the preceding Driving Lessons while completing it.

1.   Open the **Team Building Trip** message.

2.   Print three copies.

3.   Close the message.

4.   Organise all messages in your **Inbox** by **Subject** in ascending alphabetical order.

5.   Print the first message in the list.

6.   Search for any messages in the **Inbox** with the message text containing the word **team**.

7.   Search for any messages with attachments (**Advanced Find**, **More Choices** tab).

8.   Close the **Advanced Find** dialog box.

9.   Close the **Find** bar.

10. Create a new folder in the **Inbox**, called **ECDL Module 7**.

11. Move all of the messages created during this module into the new folder.

12. Sort the messages by date received, with the most recent at the top of the list.

13. Search for any messages received from yourself.

14. Print these messages, then delete them.

15. Empty the **Deleted Items** folder.

16. Close *Outlook*.

If you experienced any difficulty completing the Revision, refer back to the Driving Lessons in this section. Then redo the Revision.

Once you are confident with the features, complete the Record of Achievement Matrix referring to the section at the end of the guide.

Answers

Driving Lesson 7

Step 1   E-mail is beneficial for businesses because it is very fast, cheap and web based accounts can be accessed from any computer with Internet access.

Step 2   **Netiquette** is network etiquette: a set of rules governing how you should use e-mail.

Step 3   Messages may contain viruses.

Step 4   Make sure you have up to date anti-virus software installed. Save attachments and scan them before opening if you are suspicious.

Step 5   E-mail is electronic mail.

Step 6   An e-mail address consists of a **user name**, an **@ sign** and a **domain name**.

Glossary

Address Bar	Shows the address of the page currently displayed in the Browser and allows entry of a new address to be visited.
Attachment	Any file transmitted with an e-mail.
Distribution List	A grouping of several mail addresses than can be accessed with a single name.
Folder	A method of grouping together files (and other folders).
Forward (a message)	Send a copy of an e-mail which you have received, to another address, with an optional message of your own.
Inbox	The default folder for storing all incoming e-mail messages.
Mail Rules	Definable rules on how to treat incoming e-mails depending on certain conditions.
Outbox	The folder for storing outgoing e-mails before they have been sent.
Preview Pane	An area of the **Inbox** display screen where the contents of messages can be viewed without opening them.
Recycle Bin	An area of storage where deleted files are held temporarily before being deleted completely.
Sent Items	The folder for storing outgoing e-mails after they have been sent.
Subfolder	A folder that is contained within another folder.

Index

Record of Achievement Matrix

This Matrix is to be used to measure your progress while working through the guide. This is a learning reinforcement process, you judge when you are competent.

Tick boxes are provided for each feature. 1 is for no knowledge, 2 some knowledge and 3 is for competent. A section is only complete when column 3 is completed for all parts of the section.

For details on sitting ECDL Examinations in your country please contact the local ECDL Licensee or visit the European Computer Driving Licence Foundation Limited web site at http://www.ecdl.org.

Tick the Relevant Boxes **1**: No Knowledge   **2**: Some Knowledge   **3**: Competent

Section	No	Driving Lesson	1	2	3
1 Outlook	1	Using E-mail			
	2	Using Outlook			
	3	E-mail Help			
	4	Changing Screen Display			
	5	Message Headings			
	6	Closing Outlook			
2 Message Editing	9	Creating a Message			
	10	Cut, Copy and Paste Messages			
	11	Cut, Copy and Paste from Word			
	12	Spell Checker			
	13	Applying a Signature			
3 Send and Receive	16	Sending Messages			
	17	Open and Read Messages			
	18	Flagging a Message			
	19	Attaching Files			
	20	Open and Save a File Attachment			
	21	Changing Message Priority			
	22	Reply to / Forward Messages			
	23	Address Book			
	24	Add Sender to Address Book			
	25	Distribution Lists			
4 Message Management	29	Save a Draft Message			
	30	Printing a Message			
	31	Deleting Messages			
	32	Creating Inbox Folders			
	33	Organising Messages			
	34	Finding Messages			

Other Products from CiA Training Ltd

CiA Training Ltd is a leading publishing company, which has consistently delivered the highest quality products since 1985. A wide range of flexible and easy to use self teach resources has been developed by CiA's experienced publishing team to aid the learning process. These include the following ECDL Foundation approved products at the time of publication of this product:

- **ECDL/ICDL Syllabus 5.0**

- **ECDL/ICDL Advanced Syllabus 2.0**

- **ECDL/ICDL Revision Series**

- **ECDL/ICDL Advanced Syllabus 2.0 Revision Series**

- **e-Citizen**

Previous syllabus versions also available - contact us for further details.

We hope you have enjoyed using our materials and would love to hear your opinions about them. If you'd like to give us some feedback, please go to:

www.ciatraining.co.uk/feedback.php

and let us know what you think.

New products are constantly being developed. For up to the minute information on our products, to view our full range, to find out more, or to be added to our mailing list, visit:

www.ciatraining.co.uk

Notes